Let's Walk Home

©2024 by Alfonso Matos All Rights Reserved.

No part of this book may be used or reproduced by any means: graphic, electronic, or mechanical, including photocopying, recording, taping or by any information storage retrieval system without the written permission of the author except in the case of brief quotations embodied in critical articles and reviews. Because of the dynamic nature of the Internet, any web addresses or links contained in this book may have changed since publication and may no longer be valid. Although every precaution has been taken to verify the accuracy of the information contained herein, the author and publisher assume no responsibility for any errors or omissions so that no liability is assumed for damages that may result from the use of information contained within. The views expressed in this work are solely those of the author and do not necessarily reflect the views of the publishe whereby the publisher hereby disclaims any responsibility for them.

No part of this book may be used or reproduced by any means: graphic, electronic, or mechanical, including photocopying, recording, taping or by any information storage retrieval system without the written permission of the author except in the case of brief quotations embodied in critical articles and reviews. Because of the dynamic nature of the Internet, any web addresses or links contained in this book may have changed since publication and may no longer be valid. The views expressed in this work are solely those of the author and do not necessarily reflect the views of the publisher whereby the publisher hereby disclaims any responsibility for them.

Editor | Robbie Grayson III
Cover Designer & Interior Illustrator | Robbie Grayson III
Illustrator | Robbie Grayson III

ISBN | 979-8-8693-2598-3

Published by Traitmarker Books
www.traitmarkerbooks.com
traitmarker@gmail.com

Let's Walk Home

Alfonso A. Matos

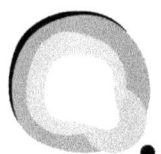

*To God for forging, protecting, and conditioning
my mind to learn from all the good,
bad, and indifferent in my life.*

*To my family for always encouraging me
to give my best, regardless of the outcome.*

*To the Dreamers like myself who follow the neverending
pursuit of an idea and boldly turn it into reality.*

*Lastly, to our children who are the future. Though life is hard
and full of uncertainty, continue to drive forward and
let present limitations curb your future.*

*"Your dreams are the preceding paths of greatness
and must be protected at all costs, because only
those who dream big can make it big."*

Alfonso A Matos | *Washington DC*

Joseph whispered to his wife, Asenath, with a sense of urgency.

"We have to move now," he said solemnly, catching her off guard. "It's not safe here anymore."

Asenath's response was immediate.

"Okay," she said with apprehension. "I wondered when this would happen. Let's tell the children."

Their children, Lydia and James, looked on with confusion when their parents sat them down.

"Why?" they asked in unison, puzzled by the sudden announcement.

Asenath's answer was unexpectedly poetic, hinting at a new beginning filled with hope and promise.

"Because we found a better place full of dreams," she explained, her words carrying a sense of excitement and possibility.

Lydia's immediate concern was for her cherished dolls, while James anxiously inquired about his beloved bicycle, unsure of what the future held for their possessions.

Joseph reassured them both to their relief, his voice a steady anchor amidst the uncertainty.

"Yes, you can. Bring it all to me, and I will carry it for you," he promised, his paternal instinct kicking in as he prepared to shoulder the burdens of their journey.

Then let's go!" the kids said excitedly.

As they stood in line, Joseph bore a heavy bag containing the children's belongings while the children's excitement bubbled over, oblivious to their father's quiet fatigue.

"It's crowded," Joseph whispered to Asenath. She patted Joseph's arm.

"We can wait. Our turn will come," she said with a patient smile.

Finally, their turn came, and they boarded the train, moving from car to car as more passengers boarded.

Eventually, the family found themselves in a crowded, less maintained car, where Joseph's weariness became increasingly apparent. And then, in a moment of quiet desperation, he decided to alter the course of their journey forever.

Stepping off the train, Joseph stood outside, his frail form illuminated by the harsh glow of the station's lights. Alarmed, Asenath found him on the platform, the children trailing behind her in confusion.

"What's wrong?"

It was then that Joseph revealed the truth of his condition.

"We can't afford to finish our journey and pay for my medicine. You must go on without me. I'm so sorry, but it's the only way."

Asenath began to cry quietly.

"Here you go. Take it," Joseph shoved the wallet with the rest of the family's money in it into Asenath's hands. "I love you. Thank you for all these years. Thank you for being a good wife. Thank you for giving me Lydia and James. Thank you for everything."

Joseph hugged Lydia.

"Grow up to be a good woman like your mom. Follow your dreams, get an education, and marry someone who will love you like I love your mother."

"Yes, Papa," Lydia said.

Joseph took James by the shoulders and looked him in the eyes.

"Be a hard worker and a good man. Protect your mother and sister. And don't forget me. You must carry the big bag now."

"Yes, Papa," James said bravely.

As the train pulled away, leaving Joseph alone on the platform, Lydia and James watched from the window, their young faces reflecting a mixture of sadness and resolve.

Asenath watched Lydia and James walk through the train cars, growing up and becoming good people. She couldn't help but to think how proud Joseph would be of both of them.

One day when Asenath was much older, she stepped off the train. Lydia and James, curious and concerned, followed her. She turned to them and gave Lydia their father's wallet.

"This is for your future. Whatever you choose to become, honor your father's and my sacrifice. Continue to make us proud as you have. This is my stop. I must get off here and leave you both to travel on your own."

Both sorrowfully hugged their mother and stepped back on the train.

One day, the train stopped. Picking up their belongings, James and Lydia both got off.

"Well," James began awkwardly. "The time has come for us to go our separate ways, sister."

Lydia blinked back her tears.

"What will you do?" she asked.

"I'm going to be a pilot in the military," James said matter-of-factly."

Lydia nodded.

"Papa would have liked that," she said quietly.

"What are you going to do," James asked Lydia.

"I'm going to university to be a surgeon," she said with confidence. "I want to help people live long, healthy lives."

James smiled.

"Mom would have liked that," James's lower lip trembled. "That's a great choice."

"Well, it's time to go." The tears were streaming down her face.

Suddenly, James took Lydia by the shoulders, just as his father once did to him. He looked her in the eyes.

"How about I join the military now and help you through medical college?"

Lydia's face brightened.

"And once I become a doctor, I'll buy us a large house while you're fighting our country's wars. When you come home, we can be together."

Both children beamed at each other for their clever idea.

"Remember how sad Papa was to leave us?" James asked. Lydia nodded.

"Remember how sad Mom was to leave us?" Lydia asked. James sighed at the thought.

"They were sad because they had to leave us. But we can make them happy and proud if we stay together."

"Exactly!" Lydia hugged her brother back. "Because the strength in family is being together!"

And that's exactly what they did!

In the end, their unwavering love for each other carried them through, binding them together as they faced the challenges and uncertainties of life's ever-changing landscape.

As they forged ahead, guided by the memory of their father's selflessness and their mother's strength, they knew that the bonds of family would always be their greatest source of comfort and courage.

About the Author

ALFONSO A. MATOS has a background in law enforcement, military consulting, and filmmaking. He is an actor, screenwriter, and executive producer known for his work on various film and television projects, including reception of the IndieFEST Film Award Recipient Nomination. Born in the Dominican Republic, Alfonso developed a passion for storytelling and filmmaking at a young age. Later, he pursued his interest in law enforcement, where he gained extensive experience in gang investigations, intervention, and military consultation, eventually becoming a renowned expert in gang and military affairs.

Alfonso is based in Washington DC, where he enjoys exploring cultural and historic landmarks, spends time with his family, and continues to write screenplays that explore the human experience. Alfonso is set to build on his success as an actor, screenwriter, and executive producer as a fresh face in the action genre. He lives by the motto, "The world is our stage. Perform!"

www.ingramcontent.com/pod-product-compliance
Lightning Source LLC
LaVergne TN
LVHW070525070526
838199LV00072B/6703